To

Love, Enjoy!

Big Daddy Graham

Last Call . . .

remembering my dad

Big Daddy Graham

To Mom, Janet, Tony, Liz
&
Debbie, Keely and Ava

Special thanks to Larry Platt who was the first to convince me that this book should "go public." He also helped with the editing along with Anthony Gargano. Kudos to Bruce Brachman whose brilliant design and layout work was inspiring. A loyal listener named Brian Kelley was instrumental with the title. Support from friends like Angelo Cataldi, Joe Conklin, John Donohoe, Bill Lyon, Mike Romano and Sal Paolantonio spurred me on to do better. Finally, without Dave Giorgio and Infinity's belief in this book, there would be no book.

Thanks!

read the intro.

My dad died on August 23rd, 1977. About a year ago I realized that the few memories I had of him were becoming very cloudy. It dawned on me that there was going to be a good chance that soon I wasn't going to remember anything at all about him.

So I bought one of those blank books and every now and then I would fill a page with some random thought or story about my dad that I still retained. If that recollection couldn't fit on a single page, I wouldn't write it. Surprisingly, every memory of him did fit on one page, and don't ask me what that says of one's life. I don't know.

Soon all the memories I had were written in the book you're holding now. I'm not sure why I did it, but I can only tell you that I would strongly suggest you do the same. I read this book all the time. It's proof that he even existed at all and it's strangely comforting. I hope some day my kids read it. My dad has been dead their entire lives and is there a chance that this book about a man they never met would help them know me better? Is that even important?

I don't know. I wrote it, you read it, then I think you should write one of your own and I'll read that, OK?

B. D. Graham, 2002

Last Call . . .

remembering my dad

We went to our first Phils game at Connie Mack. We went early for batting practice. I remember it as twilight. We were along the right field foul line, all the way back to the corner, and he caught a foul ball, a screaming line drive with one bare hand that thrusted into the air. The hand seemed huge.

Someone yelled, "sign him up" and I couldn't believe I got a ball at my first game!

Sometimes he would count to ten in Lithuanian and I think he once told me that "Taras Bulba" (a popular movie at the time) meant "big potato" in Lithuanian.

At least, that's what I told everyone it meant.

Dad's Mom and Dad

Moore's Furniture at 67th and Woodland used to be an old fashioned bowling alley where there was no automation and men would set the pins. He told me that he once had did that job.

I also heard once that for a couple days he had briefly been a paid mourner at funerals, but now I can't seem to find anyone to validate that.

He used to say that all he ever got for Christmas when he was a kid was "an orange and a piece of coal." I guess he thought Christmas had gotten too commercial, i.e., "expensive".

Anyway, one Christmas my mother got him an orange and a box of some sort of black hard rock candy that came with a little chisel. Candy that looked like coal. Cool move, mom.

He never brought up the "coal and orange" shtick again.

When I was around eight, he would hit fly balls to me at Patterson Schoolyard, which was cement. Other kids would join us and marvel. He could really hit them a mile. He did this until I was around 12 years old. Wish he never stopped.

He could also dropkick a ton. Other than a teacher I had at West Catholic, I never saw anyone else ever dropkick period.

He also played semi-pro football.

He loved Horn & Hardarts. An automated, waitressless restaurant, long since gone and never to be seen again. A really cool and strange place to a kid.

They had this weird fountain thing where you filled your own glasses of water and I remember him showing me how to use it.

I would drink glass after glass just to use this contraption.

I guess you say He was always an early riser, but I'm not exactly sure when he would sleep.

Most times you could catch him sleeping at the kitchen table along side a glass of Muskatel.

In fact I can't ever remember him ever going to bed.

However, his strange sleep habits came in handy later when as an alter boy I had to serve at the 5:15 am Mass. He'd wake me up with a big plate of scrapple (the only food he could cook) and then walk me to church.

I remember going to the zoo with him when I was eight. The zoo had these things called "zoo keys" where you bought this key and put it in this little speaker that was set up at all the exhibits.

This speaker would give you the info about whatever animal you were looking at and I wanted one of these keys. (Maybe I was 8)

My dad said that you didn't have to buy a key, you just had to "follow someone around who had one." One time, we followed this one family around for a couple exhibits and their dad gave my dad a look. My dad said "what are you looking at?"

We left right after that.

We went to Convention Hall to see the Warriors play, and he took me down to this big ramp that the players walked down from their lockers so I could stand next to Wilt Chamberlain. Afterwards we took our seats which were the third row from the top in the corner. I couldn't understand this and I remember bugging Dad. "Why can't we sit down there?"

Economics 101.

When I was in the fifth grade, I used to serve the 5:15 am Mass.

My dad would walk me in the dark and he would sometimes carry my cassock.

All the nuns went to the 5:15 am Mass. My fifth grade nun happened by chance to see my dad and I walking into the church with my dad carrying my garments. The following day, in school, this nasty nun says to me, "What's the matter? Can't carry your own clothes?"

When I told my dad about this, he called the convent and told the nun to "mind her own damn business." To this day I think my dad was the only Catholic ever to talk back to a nun and get away with it.

I was so proud.

The first little league game I ever played (the Falcons!), I walked all four of my bats, which pissed my dad off. "Swing the bat!" he told me.

Years later I yelled at my daughter Keely for the same thing.

Genes.

I remember visiting his brother who lived in a tin shack near some railroad tracks.

He was blind and dad told me someone had hit him in the head with a baseball bat when he was nine.

They sat at a formica table and drank highballs. It was summer and it was hot and I don't remember ever going back.

I only remember going to the movies with him once and for some strange reason he picked a movie that was playing at a movie house three parishes away. (Which means it might as well have been in Utah)

It was a crisp, cold day and the walk took an hour and a half.

We saw "Cimarron", a western with Glenn Ford.

He hated it and we walked the entire way home in silence.

I once called a sports talk show when I was in the 5th grade. When I was finished, my dad thought that my question was "better than any of those other idiot's questions."

This "us versus them" (or "him versus them" was more like it) was a running theme with him.

When I was 10, my dad and I would walk around the neighborhood gathering thrown away newspapers in an A&P shopping cart. We would then push it to this scrap yard where they would pay you by the pound.

We also returned bottles for cash and checked phone booths for change at the airport.

He would say that "I might get lucky, find some big businessman's wallet, turn it in and get a reward".

I often wondered just what he would have really done if I had found a wallet with hundreds of dollars in it.

But we never did.

He never went on vacation with us. In fact we never really took any "week long" vacations as a family. Mom used to take me and some friends down to Wildwood on the Jersey shore for a couple 3-day mid week jaunts a summer.

However, Dad never went and I never knew why. Maybe he couldn't afford it. Maybe he hated the shore. I never knew why.

I only remember him having one friend. A huge man with a big, drinker's nose named Bill. However, even Bill never came into our house. No one ever did.

Bill sold newspapers outside the GE factory across the street. It was through him that I got my first job ever selling newspapers. It was the summer between 5th and 6th grade. I eventually found out the whole damn newspaper thing was a front for a numbers racket that Bill ran.

Years later I got a job at the Navy Yard. The fact that Dad worked there 20 odd years didn't hurt. Weird. Here was a man without a connection in the world, and somehow I got two jobs through him.

I once got in a fight when I was in the sixth grade with this guy named "Piels" who was in the eighth. He really beat my ass.

The fight was in Patterson Schoolyard. Wouldn't you know it? Dad was walking home from the beer distributor and watched the entire thing. I think I was in five serious fights my whole life and he had to see this one. When I got home he was really pissed and told me "that I fought like a girl."

He used to call home every day at lunchtime with this ingenious method.

He'd call from the same pay phone, to which my mother had the number.

He'd ring the phone twice, which meant that he was at the phone, then my mother would call back. This saved 5 cents every day.

He never would talk to me. Or my sisters. Or my brother. Or my mother.

So I'm not sure what even the purpose of the phone call was.

He used to do most of his drinking at home, but often he would go to the bar across the street at night and drink for an hour or so.

He'd come home strolling through the living room and throw these little ten cent bags of cheese curls at me and my brother and sisters, which we would accept gleefully.

Because of this, we were always glad when he went to the bar, which I think was his plan.

I don't think it fooled my mother.

For the most part, we never had a car. However, there were two and both of them lasted a matter of months.

One of them was a used white station wagon that you couldn't enter through the passenger side because the door was tied on. He had been teaching my sister Janet how to drive and got so mad that he slammed it so hard it busted.

I remember the other short-lived used car because for some reason, my mom and dad came down to football practice to give me a ride home and it was one of the only times I ever saw my mom and dad out of the house together.

For years, I told friends that my dad had to go to the hospital once to have a rubber dart removed from his forehead.

Where in God's name did I get this story?

When my sister Janet got married, we rented this yellow car. Later that night we were coming home from this in-law party when a couple of black guys pulled up next to us. My dad thought one of them gave him a dirty look and started chasing them in our rented, yellow car with my mother screaming the entire time.

Nothing happened, but other than drinking a high ball at the reception, it's the only memory of the wedding that I have.

He drank really cheap beer. Mulheim, Stegmier, Esslinger, Ballentine. He bought it by the case in 16 oz. bottles.

He would walk to Van Zeltz beer distributor a block away and wheel the case home in one of those little grocery carts, the same one my mom would use when she went to the A&P.

I don't remember him having a favorite brand. He drank whatever was cheapest that week.

He hated black people and although I could tell a bunch of stories about that, I'd rather not.

Let's just say he came from an era and a neighborhood where that particular dislike was commonplace.

He used to walk a lot in this cool off-white raincoat, kind of like the one Columbo wears, but whiter.

If he was going to the VFW club at 58th and Woodland, he wouldn't take a trolley, he'd walk it.

I remember walking to the VFW with him, I was around eleven and I sat at this little red formica table on a tiled floor drinking cokes out of these little glasses while Dad sat at the bar. I don't think he said two words to me the entire trip, but I still loved walking with him!

He worked at the Navy yard for something like 25 years, yet to this day I have no idea what he did there. I think he unloaded trucks but he never discussed it, nor did anyone else in the family.

He was fond of saying things like "I wouldn't go see the Beatles if they were playing across the street."

Unless Betty's Luncheonette was going to start to book bands, there wasn't much chance of that.

He loved to gamble. Once, in Atlantic City, he was forced to jump out a window to escape a raid on an illegal gambling house and he broke his leg.

He still got away, though.

Mom and Dad

When Lew Alcindor changed his name to Kareem-Abdul-Jabbar, that really pissed him off. "Kareem this!" he would shout.

All the Muslim names (Muhammad Ali) really got to him.

My dad fought in the Battle of the Bulge during World War II. Not one word was ever spoken about his days in the War and it wasn't like my mom was instructing us "to never bring it up." That's just how it was.

I will say this, though. I was told dad never drank at all until he came back from the War. Plenty has been said about the various drug and social problems that faced returning Vietnam Vets. (and rightfully so)

The thing is, I always found it odd that no one seemed to point to World War II as being at least partly responsible for the millions of drunks of that generation scattered throughout the US. They saw plenty of horrors also.

In fact, I never even noticed that my dad had a drinking problem. My entire neighborhood was full of hard drinking Dads. There were a couple bars per block.

Third Row, Fourth from left

My parents got married on November 30th, 1940. This happened to be the same day as the Army/Navy football game. This duel was played in Philly and back in those days it was the ultimate sporting event of the year.

My dad had to give up two seats to the game in order to get married

They never got in a fight the rest of their lives where I didn't hear my dad say, "I should have went to the goddamned game."

He loved the word "bum." Everyone was a bum, particularly anyone who played for the Phillies or the Eagles.

"Bums!"

He used to do this weird dance move where he would bend over, wiggle his knees and criss cross his arms in front of his knees.

It looked like the "Huckle-buck" or the "Charleston". Whatever, it was the same move Jimmy Stewart does for Donna Reed in "It's a Wonderful Life."

We were always buying him back scratchers. Wooden ones, plastic ones. They were always breaking.

In my adulthood, my itchy back got so bad, I started ordering special metal back scratchers after many trips to dermatologists.

Genes.

Without question, the greatest day in my father's life (and mine also) was the day we bought a window unit air conditioner.

During the summer he used to come home from work and put his head directly on the air conditioner. Right on it!

Just for the record.

I never saw my dad kiss my mom.

I never saw my dad dance with my mom.

I never once, not once, saw my dad take my mom anywhere. Not a movie, dinner, anywhere at all.

Just for the record.

I don't ever remember seeing him in a long sleeve shirt or a tie.

Everything was always "fixed."

Sporting events.

Elections.

Life.

The word always spat out of his mouth like you were an idiot for not realizing it.

He used to "vacuum" a lot, though it really wasn't a vacuum in the electronic sense of the word.

It was this black sweeper thing. It didn't plug in or anything. It's the only chore I ever remember him doing.

He never sat in the living room with us. He always sat in the kitchen. Even if I was watching a sporting event on TV, he'd listen to the same game on the radio.

Occasionally, he would come into the living room (we'd be on the floor eating popcorn) and announce some horrible news, usually some sort of a black crime, then drift back into the kitchen.

It got to the point where we wouldn't even notice.

He always got drunk in the kitchen while listening to the radio. My sister Janet was in the Peace Corps and there was some talk radio show going on about the Peace Corps.

Apparently, my dad didn't like what the host was saying and he actually called in and started to berate them. He started using the word "Goddamned" and he got cut off and then really got pissed off.

Years later, I would have had to cut him off too.

My sister Liz was with Dad in the subway tunnels when they were approached by three punks who either said something to Liz or they wanted money.

Dad beat them all off with an umbrella.

His sister, Alice, lived two blocks away from us, but I don't recall ever meeting her.

I heard that she was a drunk. That she had nervous breakdowns. That she once jumped off the porch roof.

He was always whistling, and if you think about it, it seems like no one whistles anymore.

However, I can't seem to remember even one title he ever whistled.

The first time I ever came home drunk, I slipped and fell in the kitchen. Afraid I was caught, I looked up and my dad was snuffed out at the kitchen table, having drunk himself to sleep.

LAST CALL . . .

My brother Tony taught himself on the guitar and he could really play.

Yet Dad thought it was all a total waste of time and he used to say "he couldn't even play 'Happy Birthday' if he had to."

I was entertaining the thought of going to Woodstock when my dad saw the news coverage of the Atlantic City Rock Festival. There had been drug busts and when he saw the news, he refused to let me go.

Now I don't know if I would have gone anyway, but it was the only time where he voiced an opinion and made a decision on anything. He usually had no idea whatsoever what I was doing with myself.

Because I was Senior Class President, my dad was kind of forced to be a chaperone at my Senior Prom. As far as I remember, this was the only school activity that he ever participated in. My mom must have really laid the hammer on him to get him to go.

He ended up in an argument with a teacher who was out in the parking lot catching kids drinking. Seems he was pouring all the confiscated beer and liquor on to the ground.

My dad thought this was a waste and he split and went home about a half hour into the whole thing.

Before we had bought the window unit air conditioner, it used to get so hot that my dad would fill up the bathtub with cold water and sit in it and drink beer and listen to the Phillies on the transistor. Unopened bottles would actually float in the tub with him.

Now remember, this was a one bathroom row house that we lived in. This forced my mom to install a toilet in our crumbling basement. No fancy "powder room" or anything. Just a toilet.

When you have to go, you have to go.

How this ever happened, I'll never know, but for some reason, my dad challenged my ex-brother-in-law, who was a great Division One football player, to a game of tennis. I remember my dad leaving the house in sneaks (a first) and shorts. His legs looked ridiculous.

He got his ass kicked and almost collapsed during the game.

My dad loved Frank Rizzo. When he died, I felt like a little part of my dad died again.

With Grandkids, Dave and Kate

He never, never went out. After years of never going to the movies, he came home one afternoon complaining that he had just seen a couple movies at the Benn, and that "the movies they were making today were lousy."

Turned out he had seen a double feature of Bruce Lee Kung-Fu movies and based on these films he formed his opinion of the current state of cinema.

When I was 20, I went to this rip-off disc jockey school. Years later, the owner of this "school" ended up being arrested in a McDonald's parking lot with 30 guns in his car.

When I graduated from this "school", I had this demo tape of me doing the weather and news and I played it for everybody at home.

My dad said nothing. However, when I walked upstairs, I heard him say to my mom, "That sounds as good as any of those big shots on the radio."

He and my brother once got in a fight in the living room. The parlor was tiny and there wasn't much room for the three of us to stand in, nonetheless to throw a fight in.

It was mostly just a lot of pushing and shoving, but my dad and brother were both very large men (my brother in his early 20's) and the walls shook.

I quickly took a seat on the couch because I was afraid to move. Nothing ended up happening really and the fight evaporated, as fights tend to do.

Here's the odd thing about this story. I remember it vividly, yet my brother swears that it never happened at all.

According to my wife Debbie, the only time she ever met my dad, he told her that I had "more girlfriends than Charles Manson."

I will always believe that Deb remembers this wrong. That just does not sound like something he would have said.

To this day, however, Debbie swears to this story.

He really loved babies and he would play with a baby for hours.

The only "conversation" I ever had with my dad was on our stoop. I had an argument with mom. It was no big deal. Just an argument.

He came out and sat next to me, which he never, never did and started in on Mom.

"She's no good. She's miserable, Blah, blah, blah."

I looked at him and said it was no big deal, lighten up, and walked away.

I was 17. Had I known it was to be the only "conversation" that I would ever have with him, I would have sat there longer.

The last time I remember seeing him at my mom's, he asked me how things were going at the Navy Yard and I said "fine."

I had quit the Yard two or three years ago easy, but I never told him.

I wasn't living at home anymore and he had no idea that I had quit. The Navy Yard was miles big and you could work there for years and never bump into anyone. In fact, that was the only time I could even remember that he asked me anything about the job at all. I could have been in and out of 3 jails in that time period and would have never known.

One summer afternoon I got lucky with a local girl who let it be known to me that a sexual romp would not be out of the question.

There was one little problem. I was living in a God awful one bedroom apartment with about ten unemployed guys like myself.

So knowing my mom and dad were both working, I knew their house was empty.

Turned out I was wrong. Midway through my dad walked in on us in my old bedroom. He closed the door as quickly as he opened it.

A couple minutes later we sheepishly tiptoed down the steps and out the door. I could hear the radio on in the kitchen, so I knew he was in there.

To the day he died he never said one word about it to me.

One day after I had graduated from high school, I was cutting through the 70th Street park with some friends at about 11:30 in the morning. There was my dad sleeping on a park bench with a couple of quarts of beer underneath the bench.

Later on that day, I dropped home to do some laundry when my dad came strolling in at 5 pm. He acted like he had been at work all day having no idea that I had seen him at the park.

I said nothing and wondered how often he had done this.

Toward the end, my mom stopped giving him any drinking money. I had moved back home and had one of my endless stupid downtown jobs.

Sometimes he would be waiting for me at the corner trolley stop to bum three or four dollars off me.

He would make a big fuss about me not telling Mom. He would always pay me back, but when he died he actually owed me four dollars.

He got sick and lost seventy pounds.

In five weeks.

I remember seeing him in his boxers in the bedroom after he had lost all that weight and it really freaked me out. Supposedly the doctors told him that he would die in two years if he didn't stop drinking and sure enough . . .

When he was dying, I only went and visited him once. I remember he was sitting on the bed in one of those hospital garments.

I talked to him for a minute, then he looked at me and said, "I'm scared."

I remember two things about his wake/ funeral.

That my brother and I were cracking jokes in the car along the way to the cemetery and the driver gave us a dirty look.

The other thing was that no one came to the funeral at all.

A few years ago, I had a dream that I was performing at this comedy club in London, Ontario. (I had performed there many times) My dad was sitting in the crowd in a silver suit and white shirt and dark tie. He was laughing but there was also this serious, professional tone about him. He was impeccably groomed, which in real life, I never remember him being.

After the show he came into the dressing room and told me that he thought the show was terrific, but that the intro to a bit titled "Spam" was "dated", when in reality it was.

It was the only dream about him I ever had.

My dad had been dead for years when I was just about to be introduced to go on stage at some club. An older guy sitting at the back bar grabbed me and said, "You're Al Gudonis' son, right?"

I said, "You know my father?" and he said "sure I did."

At that very second I was introduced and when I got off stage, he was gone and no one knew who he was. Other than Bill, the man I worked for at the newsstand, I had never met anyone who said that he knew my dad.

Nobody.

When my dad died, he left absolutely nothing and I'm not just talking money. The only item whatsoever that I have of my dad's is a set of Dutch Master Playing Cards that you got when you bought a box of Dutch Master's Cigars. In fact, it was me who even bought him the cigars to begin with. Father's Days over 30 years ago.

Not a hat.

Not a car.

Not a favorite robe or sweater.

Not a baseball glove.

Not a book or a record.

Not a watch or a ring.

Absolutely nothing.

The only proof of his existence at all is this set of Dutch Master's Playing Cards.

Occasionally, I play solitaire with them.

My Dad. South Philly, 1916